PRODIGAL: A Salvation Story

Daniel Wright

Self Published with the generous help
of our Christian family 2016.

Copyright © 2016 by Daniel Wright

All rights reserved. This book or any portion thereof may not be reproduced or used in any manner whatsoever without the express written permission of the publisher except for the use of brief quotations in a book review or scholarly journal.

First Printing: 2016

ISBN 978-1-326-75877-6

Dedication

To my wife, you have always been in my corner and been my greatest champion. God blessed me by bringing you into my life and you have been my intercessor. Proverbs 31:10

To my Father, Dad you have been and will continue to be an inspiration to me. Your life's work will go on and you are an incredible human being. Matthew 25:40

To my Mother, Mum you have been there through it all and I know your heat was broken again and again. I thank you from the bottom of my heart for your fighting spirit and that you never gave up on me.

To my children, Charlotte, Morgan, Joel, Phoebe and Benjamin. I love you all so so much and I hope that my story will serve as a warning but also an inspiration to you.

To my brothers, David and Paul. I thought you would like a mention. I love you guys thank you for being there.

Contents

Foreword	12
The Early Years	14
Is 49:22	22
Fall from Grace	29
Soldier Boy	36
Internet weirdos, sex vampires & New York	44
To have and to Hold	51
Not my will, But yours!	59
Be careful what you wish for!	67
Knock Knock…..Its Jesus.	76
Hopes for the future	84
Part 2	
Dealing with the issues	90
Shame	91
Depression	97
Prayer	102

Foreword

After years of telling my story I felt prompted to actually put it down on paper.

I do not revel in the past or give any glory to my former life rather I have chosen to be inclusive of all things because I feel it is important not to short change the miraculous work God has done in my life.

I hope that this short book will help parents to be able to recognise the signs of a child on a downward spiral but also any individual who really feels that there is no way out.

There is a way out and my hope is that when reading this short story of my journey you find it.

Chapter 1 - The early Years

I have seen the best of humanity and I have seen the worst. Here is my story.

I was born early in 1979 in Colchester, Essex. My parents Fred and Maria were relatively new christians and my father christened me in the bath at home dedicating my life to God. No one in that house at that time could have known what the future would hold for any of us. Only really hoping for the best.

In the mid 80s my father was called into ministry and as a family we packed up our house and moved to Surrey so he could attend bible college and become a minister. My memories of that time are full of joy. We lived in the countryside next to a stately home with views of fields and cows. I had no worries and was a happy child. This experience would be one that I would look back at fondly for the rest of my life especially in the dark times.

After completing his study we moved back to our home town of Colchester where my Dad took up a position as a pastor of a church. My own journey with God would begin shortly after. After a short while the church my father pastored joined into a another local church. This church had vision and God was truly working through it for the town we lived in. The church was one of very few in the UK that had its own school. It was at this school that I would form a friendship with a remarkable young man called N.

We were firm friends from the outset and spent our time playing and reading and generally being boys. One summer afternoon while out playing near a farm that N's family were living at I had my first experience of God's hand on my life.
We were heading home after a busy afternoon messing about near some hay bails we came to an empty road. Just about to

cross we couldn't There right in front of us was the biggest man I had ever seen. Standing taller than a house, clothed in white and carrying a huge sword and shield, he smiled at us with a peaceful smile. As a car appeared from nowhere speeding down the country road it only just missed hitting us because this man was in the way protecting us both from what would have been death. We had seen an angel. To this day I have never seen another.

I remember running all the way back to my friends house and telling my parents. They knew instantly that we had not only been saved but also that God really had his hand on our lives. This was the first but it would not be the last time that my life was nearly snatched away.

Church life was good, I had at age 8 made a decision to become a christian and read my bible daily. I looked forward to church and believed that my little band of friends would go on to change the world.

Our house was always filled with theological discussion, people visiting who needed advice or help and my parents were always there for anyone who needed them. Today when I reflect on this I am truly grateful for my parents who did all they could to help anyone. However in my teenage years I would grow to resent them for it.

My christian experience from ages 8-13 was actually incredible. The young people of our church were so blessed by the youth workers we had. These few people cared for us, taught us and were always there for us. We would have prayer meetings on Sunday mornings and there would be healing and prophesies. These young children laying hands on there pals and seeing change. These young people were not afraid to talk to anyone about Jesus and what a difference he could have in their lives. I remember clearly our youth workers reaching out into a local council estate and working with the young people from difficult backgrounds and bringing them to salvation. Incredible times. It was this experience that would start a life long love for working with young people.

So many times in my youth my friends and I were prayed over and such powerful words spoken over us about being pastors in our own right or reaching out into the world. This group of young people were going to change the world. This group of young people were a prize to fought over by the enemy, and how he fought!

Chapter 2 - Is 49:22

Throughout this time my Father became involved in Aliyah (the biblical return of the Jewish people to Israel) related ministries (he continues to do so today). As such my summer holidays were a little different to most people my age. Between 1988 and 1992 I traveled with my parents all over Eastern Europe visiting others who were getting ready for Communism to fall and the borders to open to allow the Jewish people who had been oppressed for so long. To read more on this "A Banner to the Nations" By Fred Wright is highly recommended. (Shameless plug). Throughout my travels we built a farm, helped Jewish people escape persecution, spent time in synagogues, met with Jewish leaders and even got lost in Transylvania, the latter I would not recommend to anyone.

One memory I would really like to share with you is our visit to Majdenek. Majdenek is a concentration camp located just outside Lublin in Poland. Even at an early age I knew what the Holocaust was but while horrid nothing could have prepared me for seeing it up close an personal.

The camp was an eerie place although a warm day I felt cold as we walked through the gates. Perhaps it was fear or perhaps it was that I was actually seeing the worst that humankind could do. The first building we entered was the gas chamber. In itself it was nothing more than a building. What chilled me to the bone was that right in the centre there was an air tight "viewing" room. How could anyone want to watch thousand of innocent people die in such a horrific way. Something was stirring in my spirit even then. A righteous anger of sorts. The next building was an accommodation hut that was floor to ceiling full of spectacles. The enormity of the number of people who had been murdered there hit me so hard that my mum had to take me out of the camp as I could no longer go on in there.

This moment is when I promised myself I would always stand up for those who couldn't stand up for themselves. Just writing this now remembering this experience has me in tears. Some years later I would return to Majdenek and view the whole camp. Although I felt the same I wanted to honour the memory of so many who had perished and again made my promise I would always stand up for those who needed it. From those years to date my parents have been involved in the return of over two hundred and fifty thousand Jewish people to Israel from Eastern Europe and Ethiopia.

Some years later on a trip to Romania we had the privilege to visit a local synagogue. The caretaker, an elderly jewish man let us in showed us around. It was an extraordinary building that had survived the war. We asked if we could pray with him and I noticed that he did not have a Kippah (traditional jewish male head covering). As we had travelled to many places like this I owned one and would always wear it when visiting such a place. I asked him why he didn't have one. He told me that they were very expensive and even more had to come by. I gave him mine. He broke down in tears and told me it was the kindest thing that anyone had ever done for him. The impact of this would not really hit me until much later in life. That just a small kind gesture can make all the difference in someones life. I have held on to this belief ever since.

My own love of the Jewish people has never wained over all these years. Today I am again involved in some small part educating believers in their role in the return of God's people, the rise of Anti Semitism and what we can do about it.

Chapter 3 - Fall from Grace

When I was thirteen the christian school closed I went to a secular school in my home town. What a culture shock it was. The people I associated with, whilst generally good people were not Christians and as such I found myself moving further and further away from God.

The fact that I was, at this point, a Christian was of great entertainment to my new social crowd. This is where the bullying would start and my first desire to fit in no matte what the cost. I think that today we all talk a good game about bullying and how we should be on our guard to negate it in school and the like but the truth of the matter is that if someone really wants to hurt you they will. It will always come when there is no one to stand up for you, or when you are at your lowest.

I suppose today what I find most interesting is that my social justice compass was still very active but my moral one was clearly not working. That year so many things happened that attributed to what would become many years of turmoil and destructive behaviour.

I was still very innocent in the ways of the world and really had no understanding of how much influence the little things would make in my life. For a few months my behaviour outside of the family was just plain naughty, going out on my bike and getting into bits of trouble. I still felt convicted though of my behaviour and would always feel ashamed. Shame however would really do a number on me shortly after Christmas 1992 when I went to my first non christian party. It was here I discovered alcohol and lost my innocence. I was so ashamed of what had happened and didn't know how to handle it. I really didn't feel that I could talk to anyone about it. After all to my non Christian friends I was a bit of legend but on the inside I felt awful. It wouldn't be long before I began to get into the drug scene. The drugs numbed the sense of shame for a short while but I felt more and more distance from my parents and from God.

Between 1993 and 1995 I had a string of promiscuous relationships, took more drugs and drank a lot. I managed to keep the majority of this hidden from my parents. I wanted to feel wanted and loved. I should point out that I was wanted and so loved by my parents. I just didn't love myself. I looked for love in sex and having lots of "friends" around me. I was on a downward spiral and something had to change. I didn't look to God for the change, in fact I looked the completely other way and became obsessed with the occult. I now believed in all things dark. I played with ouija boards, read books on spells and paganism. By May 1995 I had finished my exams, most of which I was high when taking. The occult wasn't working for me either. Every day was the same. Wake up. Take drugs. Find someone to sleep with. Take drugs. I was going to die if things didn't change. Because of the way I was living I was full of hate for all things Church and all things Christian. I couldn't bear to be in the house with worship music being played, people praying and listening to how God loved everyone. It all had to be lies right? I mean how could God love me. I was damaged goods and not worth loving, or so I thought. I had to get away from it all and did the only logical thing I could think of. The war in the former Yugoslavia had started and I wanted in. Worst case scenario I would get away from home, best case scenario I would catch a bullet and that would be the end of it. It was hard work but I came off the drugs and cleaned up my act just enough to gain entry into the British Army.

Chapter 4 - Soldier Boy

September 1995 I joined the Royal Corps of Signals and moved away from home to a training regiment. I was excited by this and gave it my all. However in the quiet moments I found myself longing for home and considered leaving the Army a few times. I wrote home asking for money and asking if my parents would get me out. They couldn't and I stayed in. Resolved to make this life change worthwhile I worked hard at soldiering and became proficient in all things. Work time I was a good soldier. Down time I was boarder line alcoholic and sex addict. Weekends were a blur of alcohol and meaningless sex. I would soon be diagnosed with depression and worse I would attempt to end my own life. Not because I couldn't handle my job it was now what I lived for, it was that I couldn't handle myself. I was, in my eyes, worthless. I had become void of feeling and longed for death. One event would push me over the edge.

I had always considered myself as a fully licensed heterosexual and as such in a very masculine environment all things

"Gay" were a source of ridicule. One particular evening after perhaps one beer too many I found myself in a situation that would rock the foundations of identity. I had crossed the line and snogged a mate all for the banter. However it was anything but banter, I began to feel some arousal. This was a shock. The shock turned to shame very quickly and worse yet caused me to spiral into a lifelong battle with depression. For the six months following the incident I questioned my identity daily. Was I gay? I'd had girlfriends all my life so perhaps I was Bi? More so if I was gay how would I live in an environment where that lifestyle was generally not accepted? What would my parents say? Being the son of a Pastor how would my parents take it? Would they be ashamed of me? I felt that notion of being gay was wrong as it was certainly a belief I had grown up with.

Those six months were the part of the worst moments of my life, in which after taking anti depressants and seeing a counsellor, whom I had not really told what my issues were found me taking an overdose of prescribed medication in what would become the first of a few failed suicide attempts. My military friends smuggled me out of camp to get medical help so it wouldn't go on my personal record. This enabled me to remain a soldier. However there was an after effect of this. The nightmares came and would remain with me every night until October 2014.

Being a logical person I eventually came to the conclusion that the mix of being around people whose lives I had vowed to protect and whom I loved in my own way, alcohol and loneliness produced the arousal and ultimately it was a yearning to feel loved. I came to this conclusion as I had realised that I actually didn't fancy men in my day to day life.

All the while one thought remained regardless, how could anyone love me. How could anyone really love a failure, a drunk, who could really help me. I left regular service in December 1999. I returned to the family home and continued my downward spiral. Every day was an excuse to get drunk, to sleep around and to take drugs. A new acquaintance had introduced me to cocaine. For the brief time that the cocaine coursed around my body I could forget how much I hated myself. I was a failure and worthless in my own mind. I was a mess. I would get home in the early hours of the morning trying to avoid sleeping. I was so scared of my nightmares that I would do anything to stay awake sometimes for days at a time. I would wake screaming covered in sweat calling for my mum. Whilst at my parents house she would run to me and all I could do was beg in tears that she would pray for me. She would stay with me until I finally fell asleep. Another failed suicide attempt came and daily I prayed for death.

Chapter 5 - Internet Weirdos, Sex Vampires and New York

I had recently discovered the internet and something called chat rooms. I fell quickly into a weird fantasy world of people who actually believed they were real life vampires. To start I found it comical, people to ridicule and a source of amusement until that is I started to get into it. My knowledge of the occult appealed to some of them and I was invited to New York by a woman who had professed her love for me and all things dark. I felt that this was an opportunity not to be missed. Looking back on it now it is absolutely ridiculous to think that it was safe or normal.

In my hatred of all things Christian and my willingness to escape I acquired the funds by nefarious means and that day I was on a flight to New York.

Landing in New York I honestly had no idea what I was getting into. Im not sure who was more surprised by my arrival, me or the people I was going to see. I arrived in rough part of Queens around midnight. My hosts although surprised welcomed me in. This was to be the most dangerous and self destructive month of my life. Sex, drugs and the occult are not a great mix. These people lived a life of drugs and sexual occult activity I involved myself with all of it, after all I wanted to die and it seemed like a half decent way to go. The nightmares grew more and more vivid every day Like falling through a rabbit hole it didn't take long for me to be looking back up towards the ever dwindling light and wondering how I had ended up here. I was scared. very scared.

Every time I thought I could be able to break away from it someone new to sleep with, more drugs, more occult, more drinking. I had Within a week or so I was sleeping on the floor of a crack den and literally had no hope left in my life. I was desperate, for the first time in years I called out to God. I knew I had to call my family. I managed to get some money together to make a phone call home to my parents. I was truly broken. I asked their forgiveness which they gave and the next day I was flying home. I had lost so much weight and looked gaunt. I knew that the only thing left was to ask God to help me.

Landing in the UK my parents were heartbroken not only at who I had become but what had happened to me.
We went straight from the airport to a meeting my Dad was speaking at. That was the day I met my wife. More on that later.

After being back in the UK for a few days my parents took me to see a pastor and close friend who had lots of experience in praying for people who had been involved in the occult. It was a most surreal experience, I suppose I was expecting some kind of violent manifestation like in the Exorcist but none came. In fact the opposite, I felt lethargic and fatigued instead but afterwards I felt lighter in my soul. From this point I started to remember that God was indeed real. Although I made no recommitment at this stage I certainly had a belief in God.

Chapter 6 - To have and to Hold

Later that year I had the opportunity to spend time with a wonderful ministry that was travelling around churches in the UK spreading the message of Aliyah. My now wife was part of a prophetic dance troupe. It was on this trip that our romance blossomed and even Tristan and Isolde had nothing on us (thats our opinion anyway). We were engaged whilst mid trip and in the August we were married. Natasha (my wife or the Boss as she is called in our house) told me that when praying about marrying me God told her that her job was to love me no matter what. This mission that God gave her would prove to be the hardest thing she has ever done.

We went to church together every week and after a short while my own feelings toward church dwindled rapidly. I had not really committed my life to God but rather was slightly grateful for the help after New York. As time passed we were expecting our first child, a girl. Charlotte came into the world with some minor complications and while the doctors were doing what they do best I was overcome with fear that we would loose her. I remembered my promise to look after those who couldn't look after themselves and for the first time in what seemed like forever I offered up a sincere prayer that God would save our daughter. He did.

Once out of the woods I remember holding this beautiful little girl in my arms and looking out of the hospital window. I made another promise. I told her that no matter what happened in life, no matter what choices she made I would always love her and I would never ever let anything happen to her. In that moment something inside me changed. I knew now that I had to live my life for my little family.
However I still had a secret that no one knew. I was battling every day against severe depression and suicidal thoughts. The Devil was really doing a number on me. I would look at my daughter and start to believe that I was not good enough to be her father, that I would never be able to make her happy. It got so bad that secretly I had turned back to drink.

On the face of it all we had the perfect life. A good job, a nice house, plenty of money we were set. But behind the scenes I began to believe that they would have a better life I wasn't around. This is where the cracks began. Two years later Morgan our eldest son was born. I was so happy to have this little boy in our lives there was a brief reprieve in the depression. Sadly it didn't last. It became harder and harder to hide my secret depression. It was now worse. The negative thoughts grew worse. How could these children love me when I felt like the world would be a better place without me. less than a year later our second son Joel was born. Whilst completely overcome with love for my own children I believed that I would ruin their lives. I want to make it perfectly clear to all who are reading this that and especially my children that being a father was not the cause of my depression and I love all my children dearly and are one of my greatest reasons to live and to share my story.

By this time we had been married for five years and my secret began to take a toll on our marriage. My dosage of anti depressants was at the highest it had been, I was drinking daily and when I thought I could get away with it the drugs made a reappearance in my life. I couldn't bear to be at home where I thought I was only a minute away from suicide. All I knew was that I couldn't be in the house like that because I wouldn't want my family to have to deal with it. I moved out for a while and we were heading for divorce. Natasha couldn't take it anymore and I just wanted to die.

Natasha flew home to Ukraine to speak to her family about what was about to happen. While she was away my parents knew that it was all but the end for us. They continued to pray and asked me if perhaps I would like to join them in Israel for a short break to clear my head. Being one of my favourite destinations in the world I said yes. In my heart knowing that when I came back I would finally kill myself. I owed them that time together as penance for all I had put them through.

God, however had a very different plan.

Chapter 7 - Not my will but yours!

Just before flying out Natasha asked me to place a folded up prayer she had written into the Western Wall. I agreed and didn't give it a second thought. We flew out to Israel on the short break and on landing I was feeling a little ill with the flu. We went to a chemist and bought some standard meds. They helped for the period of the break.

A few days of spending time with my parents was pleasant but all the while I knew this would be the last time and I was determined to put on a great act so that they would only have fond memories of me. One afternoon we walked to the old city and as we approached an elderly Chassidic man approached me and asked if I would like to donate some loose change so some cause or another. I don't know why but I handed him a 10 shekel note and he was nearly in tears. He firmly grasped my hands and told me that I was a Tzaddik (righteous man). In my mind and in my heart I was anything but righteous.

I made my way down to the wall and admired it for a short while.

I remembered that I had Natasha's prayer in my pocket. It was sealed in an envelope and I didn't see the point in being nosey so I wedged it into a little crack. It was at that moment I remember thinking right if I pray anywhere this has got to be the best place to do it. After all I had nothing to loose. "Right then God, if you are real and you actually care about someone as worthless as me. Show me".

I had one of those moments you only ever hear about, no sooner as the last word left my lips I felt a great force upon me like standing under a waterfall of light. I felt clean, I knew instantly that I was of worth and he said to me "I love you no matter what, you have a job to do for me and I will be with you all the way." I fell to my knees and wept for what seemed like an eternity. God had spoken to me, me who was a wretch, me who wanted to waste my life, me who was nothing. I walked away from the wall towards my father. He embraced me warmly and simply said "I know".

My whole life changed in an instant, there was no suicidal thoughts, I knew that although not perfect I could be a great dad and husband. My mother was elated. I couldn't wait to tell Natasha about how God had met me days before I would have ended my life and had taken away all my pain. We flew back a few days later. On the flight back I was feeling really quite sick. We got home around midnight and Natasha and I stayed up the whole night talking about what God had done. We cried together at his amazing love and I apologised for all I had put her thought we knew that God had put us together for a reason. She told me just before I went to work that her prayer that I squeezed into that crack in the wall wasn't for her or for the kids just simply that God would save me. I love my wife so much but what a character she has putting me before herself even in her hardest times. I am truly blessed.

I went into work in the morning on a day like another, except it wasn't a day like another I was alive! Towards the end of the day my manager told me that although happy I looked really ill and insisted I went to the doctors. I made my way the last appointment of the day. The doctor worked me up and asked how I was feeling. I said I felt good. I told me I shouldn't as my temperature was 41.5 degrees and in theory I should be dead. My life was about to change again.

Chapter 8 - Be careful what you wish for!

I could hear the sirens of the ambulance before my eyes came into focus, there was a hot searing pain in my chest and the the medic was asking me if I could hear him, shining a light in my eyes it became apparent all to quickly that something not ideal was happening to me. I began to loose my vision and hearing again I was slipping away.

It turns out that my heart gave out in the doctors surgery and I was clinically dead for 4 minutes until the paramedics got there and put me on the defibrillator. In the ambulance my heart gave out again this time I was gone for 7 minutes as the medical team worked on me. I want to be able to tell you that I saw a white light and the gates of heaven. The cold truth of it is I didn't see anything I didn't feel anything except pain. Reflecting on that now I have come to the conclusion that it was not my time to go and there was a real battle going on for my life.

I was out of it for a couple of days and on regaining consciousness I did what all men do on waking and decided to go for a pee. I put my feet on the floor, stood up and promptly hit the deck like a sack of the proverbial. The nurses ran to me and helped me up chastising me greatly for me endeavour to relieve myself. They asked why I fell and the horrifying realisation hit me. I couldn't feel my legs. The doctors came quickly and poked and prodded me, shining lights in my eyes. They were unsure but evil reports were being thrown around like Transverse Myelitis, Gillian Barrie syndrome or worse yet Multiple Sclerosis. A lumbar puncture was in order so they told me. Within half an hour a team of medical people surrounded me. They explained that I had to hold still or there was a risk of paralysis as they plunged the needle into my spinal cord. However they reassured me that I wouldn't feel anything except a little pressure as the anaesthetist would numb the outer areas of the skin. If only he had managed to do it. I felt the whole thing and let me tell you it hurt. A lot. As the needle hit my spinal cord I cried out and vomited. They couldn't complete the procedure. The consultant decided the the hospital I was in couldn't deal with case like mine and I was flown to a larger hospital in a neighbouring city.

Arriving at the main hospital I was taken to the twelfth floor where they hosted all the neurological terminally ill patients. I remained composed at this time. A doctor came to see me, short, dressed in a 3 piece suit he told me that they had to do a lumbar puncture right then. After some negotiation for a cigarette and a wheelchair to go downstairs and smoke it I finally agreed. The lumbar puncture went off without a hitch. The next day I was told that I had Acute Viral Encephalitis, this illness has a mortality rate of 80% if untreated and by there calculations I had been unrelated for nearly 3 weeks. However I looked promising and they set me on a course of steroids.

A few days later my condition deteriorated critically. I could no longer feel my hands, my sight had completely gone from my left eye, my hearing was drastically impaired and I could no longer speak properly. A few more days and my short to medium term memory was shot to bits. I was now trapped inside my mind and the depression tried to flood me so I would give up and die. God however kept whispering a verse to me from Joshua 1:9 *"Have I not commanded you? Be strong and courageous. Do not be frightened, and do not be dismayed, for the Lord your God is with you wherever you go."* I knew that God had my back, he didn't save me just so I could die languishing in hospital bed mere weeks later. I held firm to this.

My condition got worse still over the next few days and one morning the doctor came to me, his face solemn. He told me that the way the illness was progressing I would within the next few days slip into a coma and then die. God continued to remind me of the passage in Joshua and our time together at the wall.

My mother refused to accept the doctors report and and even told him outright "I don't accept that, in Jesus name." She would tell me everyday that I would be home soon and we would have our own little party, this reminded me of as a youth when Dad was away, or I had been bullied and was feeling generally down. She would say, "Never mind son, we will have our own little party." I am eternally grateful for those times.

My parents always said I was as stubborn as a mule. I remained so on this occasion and prayed and prayed and prayed. The coma never came. The next months were the most difficult of my life. Every day was a fight to stay alive. I had something to live for not just my family but God's promise to me that he had a job for me. The times when family visited were especially hard as I literally dint not recognise my own children this was especially painful and difficult for them as it was for my wife.

Six months and two weeks later I was released to my parents care with the prognosis that I would never walk again and at best I might be able to hold small conversations. At this point I was wheel chair bound and not able to speak properly or read.

God continued to stay close to my side and remind me that he was there with me no matter what.

The change of environment and the continued prayers of friends and family made a huge change to my life. God had not only saved me at the wall but he had saved my actually life again. Within a few weeks I was shuffling about on a zimmer frame, a couple of weeks more onto crutches, few more then onto a walking stick. Two weeks later I was home with my wife and wonderful children.

Chapter 9 - Knock Knock, its Jesus

The next couple of years saw us move to back to our home county of Essex and the birth of our second daughter Phoebe and 18 months later the final arrow of my quiver Benjamin. I found a great job in the city, I had a fantastic and rewarding hobby as a professional youth worker for a government initiative all was well in the world but something was missing. The years passed and nothing much had changed we went to church and generally lived our lives.

October 2014 and life was grand except one thing I had started to feel the familiar pangs of depression creeping in. One evening whilst having drinks in London and a small tiff with Natasha I had decided to stay in the city as it was late. In my hotel let out a half heart prayer, well not so much a prayer more like a moan. This was the night I was to realise I was not a young man anymore. After all young men see visions and old men dream dreams.

I saw a stage. a stage with me on it. a stage with me on it and people laughing. Briefly I thought ok so I am going to be comedian but the fear came over me. A Pastor…..no thank you!

The same evening God had put me on Natasha's heart and by her own admission she really didn't want to pray for me. Man I love that woman! She began to intercede on my behalf and prayed for hours. God told her she would be a Pastors wife. A few days later while working I prayed about this dream begging God not to send me into ministry. He answered me as clearly as the day he saved me from the brink of suicide. He told me to leave my job and pick apples.

I was adamant that I would not be quitting my job. He told me that it wasn't my choice anymore. That day I had a cluster headache and it floored me. I had to leave work for the hospital to get checked out. They signed me off for a week and work was not gracious at all. I was told to back at my desk the next day or kiss my job goodbye. This was a shock as I was a personal friend of the director and it was he that offered the ultimatum. I went to go in the next day feeling fine and God reminded me that I was to do as he asked and I had another of these cluster headaches.

I didn't need telling twice. I quit my job that day and never looked back. A few weeks later a man knocked on the door and asked if anyone was interested in a job picking apples. How funny God is. I had quit my very well paid and well respected job in a top company to pick apples for minimum wage.

Getting ready one morning for the days labour and feeling particularly narked that it seemed God's plan was for me to pick apples I challenged God just like I did at the wall. "God, why? Is this really what you want for me? How do I even know that this is right? I won't believe this is you unless I see the holes in Jesus hands for myself!." I walked into my bedroom to get dressed and right there Jesus approached me hand held open wide for me to see. I reached out and held onto his hands and saw the sadness in his eyes that I had, had to come to this. I fell to my knees and wept. How could I question God's plan. Out picking apples day after day I prayed for the the next step, I prayed for family, I prayed for friends I prayed and prayed and prayed. Finally God released me from apple picking to go to Bible College to study theology in a youth context.

My time in the orchards taught me valuable lessons in humility, worship, prayer but above all how to put my full trust in God.
At the time of writing I am just starting my second year.

Chapter 10 - Hopes for the future.

It has been a long hard and painful struggle to get where I am today. I could not have done it with out raising my arms and and asking to be saved. God took me from the brink of suicide, infirmity, divorce, drug and alcohol abuse and told me he loved me. He loved me so much that he gave up his most precious thing, the thing he loves more than anything and allowed his own son to die on my behalf so I wouldn't have to.

I have fought depression and won. However I could never have defeated it without God in my corner and the intersession of my wife and parents. I remain committed to God and his call on my life. I am ready to go where he will send me. I am ready to speak to those who know what it feels like to want to die. I am ready to help others conquer drug and alcohol addiction with the most powerful rehab available to man. The Gospel. I look forward to the day that my wife and I are pastoring a church and making our lives available to those who need it. We are so ready to go the unwanted and make them wanted. We are not doing this on our own. God is in our corner, he has our back no matter what.

Most importantly he has your back too. It doesn't matter who you are, it doesn't matter where you are from, what food you eat, what you have done in your past. It doesn't matter who you think you are. What matters is that God loves you as much as he loves me. What matters is that no matter how bad you think you are he loves you with all his heart. What matters is that where others see failure he sees possibility. Where others see death, he brings life. All you have to do is ask. Just raise your hand to him and let him welcome you home. Let God bring you home to his house. A house of love and care. There is always room at the table for you.

I was the son who left.

I was the son whom he welcomed back with open arms and loved me no matter what.

I am the the Prodigal.

I have seen the best of humanity and I have seen the worst. This was my story.

Part 2 - Dealing with the issues.

Shame.

Shame can be debilitating and life changing sometimes for the good but predominately for the bad.

In this section I will look at how I felt, what the bible says and what you can do about it and ultimately my hope is that it will change your perspective on this issue.

The sensation of shame as mentioned earlier engulfed me at an early age as result of doing something that I believed to be wrong. It started within my own thought process. I knew that my actions would be a disappointment to God and my parents and although convicted that I had crossed the line I kept it hidden, in my own way I thought I could even hide it from God if I didn't engage him in anyway.

Proverbs 18:3 says "When wickedness arrives, shame's not far behind;..." So the bible tells us that when we do something wicked in the eyes of God shame follows in rapid succession. So we must question is shame from God or is it the product of living an ungodly lifestyle. I would suggest that shame is of the enemy and a byproduct of the act. Simply put whilst doing whatever it is you may well enjoy, the price we pay is shame and as such it is a heavy price. Now of course there is the exception to the rule around individuals who feel shame because of something bad that has happened to them. However the mode of delivery of the shame sensation is the same. We all believe it is our fault whether actual or supposed.

Self loathing comes into the equation here too. Once we accept that the shame is a consequence of our own actions real or supposed we begin to doubt our self worth. For example in my own struggles once shame had a firm hold I never believed I would be good enough. Good enough for what? It didn't matter, all that mattered was that I wouldn't make the grade whether academically, in relationships or for God.

Shame will stop you from realising your true potential, it will cripple your relationships stopping you from having fulfilment. Shame will send you down into a dark place where depression can and will take hold.

One of the other byproducts of shame is guilt again either actual or supposed. When we feel guilt it can be debilitating. Guilt leads to repression, depression, self harm and overcompensation of the moral compass. Overcompensation of ones moral compass can and often does reveal itself in fear of rejection , again actual or supposed.

Over the last 13 years working with various youth organisations what I have come to realise is that young people today suffer so much shame and guilt over their actions. I recently had to write a case study about sexting and I was not surprised to read that those who had engaged in that activity suffered massively from shame and guilt. In a world where your every move and feeling is broadcast on social media, "likes" are golden. A lack of likes equates to rejection and ultimately fear of rejection. Our society has created an environment that individuals are constantly scrutinised over looks, politics, opinions, gender and sexuality. As such young people are in the crosshairs daily where one comment can send them into a very bad place.

If you accept these thoughts as a result of shame you are on a very slippery slope indeed. It is important to remember that you are God's creation Psalm 139:14 reminds us "I praise you, for I am fearfully and wonderfully made…". It is of course very hard to remember that we are made that way. So I would suggest to you that God created you for the sole purpose of hanging out with you and spending time with you. Thats right, you!
God wants to speak to you, fellowship with you and fight your corner. Why? because he made you. Think about a time in your own life where you have accomplished anything it really doesn't matter what it is. Remember the feeling of pride you had in that moment. Now think on this. God feels like that every time he looks at you, his perfect creation.

What can you do about it? thats the question. Firstly you need to verbalise your shame to God. Speak to God and express your shame to him. If you aren't a believer this is as good as a time as any to offer up a prayer. Jesus died for you. He died for me. He died for us all. Not because it seemed like a good idea but because God loves you warts and all. When Jesus died all those years ago he took your sins and SHAME upon himself so that you no longer have to suffer but can be saved and be free from it. This is your opportunity to be free. At the back of the book there is a short prayer that you can say and ask God to save you. If you are reading this and thinking what on earth is this guy on about, let me put it in the simplest way I can. We all need to be saved from something no matter how small or large, like drowning, we put our arms up and pray for someone to save us from death. Put your hands up and be saved.

Secondly find yourself good people that you can talk to about your shame, share your story, you will be surprised by how many other people can relate to what you are going through.

One of my military instructors once said "Ask questions, remember there are no stupid questions, only people stupid enough not to ask when they are in trouble." Reach out for help when you need it most.

Thirdly, you have nothing to be ashamed of. No matter what is in the past, Today is Today. Today is the start of something new. If you feel the shame creeping back in read John 3:16 " For God so loved the world, that he gave his only son, that whoever believes will not perish but have eternal life."

Depression.

Here is a big one and I don't profess to have all the answers on this one at all but I know a man who does!

You will have read how I spent most of my life knocking back anti depressants, alcohol and drugs to elevate my own depression. The journey through that was of course difficult and really in this part I am hoping that those of you who are blessed enough not to have had depression will have a greater understanding of those who do. To those of you out there who are fighting this right now I have some encouragement for you too.

Depression must be viewed as symptom not a cause, finding the cause of the depression, perhaps shame, fear of rejection, actual rejection, loss or confusion is paramount for both those on the outside and those suffering. The way we view depression must change. It can no longer be seen as something that is a root cause rather it is the symptom of underlying issues.

Imagine if you will, waking in the morning and the first thought you have is to go back to sleep. Not because your bed is all cosy and warm or that its your day off. Rather because the thought of facing another day floods your eyes with tears. Because knowing that you will have to put on a mask to the outside world and pretend that everything is ok. Now think about sitting alone perhaps reading, but the only thoughts you have are of having to face another day, or being alone. Now imagine that, that is how you think all day, every day and you cant remember the last time you were happy. I am sure you will have read or seen Harry Potter at some time. There are these nasty creatures in that suck all your happiness out of your soul. That is what depression feels like.

Now you know, how will you treat those around you that seem maybe a little distant? or perhaps a little detached? or those who always seem sad?

Depression can and does lead to suicide and those of you out there that think suicide is a just a cry for help, you may be right, but I put it to you that when a person feels like the only way out is death its not a cry for help, its a cry for an end to torment.

Now God does not want us to live a life of sadness and depression, God wants us to live, to the fulness of life. His plan for you is not one of anxiety and woe. Think back to the shame section. God wants to live with you and in you. He wants the best for you. The bible calls us to be joyful and full of praise Phillipians 4:4 "Rejoice in the Lord always and again I say rejoice."

What can you do about it? Well if you don't suffer from depression then I urge you to treat everyone a little more carefully. You never know that one kind word may well be what stops someone from taking their own life. Try and be a bit more understanding of other peoples situations and issues after all do you ever really know what someone else is going through.

If you suffer from depression let me encourage you. If you are reading this then you are a fighter, you are a survivor and you have not yet given up. You have it in you to stay the course and be strong. I know from my own experience that it is by no means easy to shrug it off. I also know that I didn't get through it alone. You have made it this far and God sees that. He sees you. He is waiting for you talk to him, he is waiting to take away your depression. It may seem that there is no point in even bothering to try and talk to God. Let me tell you my brave fighters, there is every point in talking to him. There is a great song called "Good, Good Father." The words are beautiful but more importantly it reminds us that no matter what we do indeed have a good good father who wants the best for you.

Reach out to him today, call out to him and remember you are not as broken as you think. Being broken is an uncomfortable place to be but God can build you back up and your experiences are no less valid as anyone else.

Prayer

Father,

I know that you know me and that you want the best for me,

I thank you for your love and that you made me,

I ask your forgiveness for all that I have done that is displeasing to you and I thank you that Jesus took on all my pain at the cross so that I could be free.

I ask you to fill my heart with your love and I welcome you into my life.

You are a Good Good Father.

In Jesus name.

Amen.